SUPER SEXY GOAL SETTING

The Fun and Simple Goals Strategy to Create a Life You Love

-A *Nourish Your Soul* Book-

Julie Schooler

Copyright © 2018 Julie Schooler, BoomerMax Ltd

ISBN: 978-0-473-44623-9

All rights reserved. No part of this publication may be reproduced, distributed, or transmitted in any form or by any means, including photocopying, recording, or other electronic or mechanical methods, without the prior written permission of the publisher, except in the case of brief quotations embodied in reviews and certain other non-commercial uses permitted by copyright law.

DISCLAIMER

This book is designed to give the reader (that means YOU – the sexy person reading this!) some useful tips and ideas about how to create and act upon your personal goals list. It has suggestions for goals, but every reader is ultimately responsible for selecting the goals that best suit him or her. Goals may pose some risk. The author and publisher advise readers to take full responsibility for their safety. What this means for YOU:

- Talk to a health professional before embarking on any increased physical activity.
- Make sure you have full and correct insurance (travel, health, etc.) whenever required.
- Use common sense to keep safe when traveling locally or abroad, and research safety measures that are appropriate in other countries or regions.
- Make sure any equipment you use has been well-maintained.
- Choose reputable companies with the best safety records.
- Tell someone where you are going, what you are doing, and when you expect to be back.
- Choose goals that are within your means financially or for which you are prepared to budget and save.
- Make responsible arrangements so that your work, family and other important areas of life remain in good condition while you pursue your goals.

Please, please, please do not choose irresponsible, destructive or illegal items for your goals.

The author and publisher accept no responsibility for any harm or loss resulting from your pursuit of your goals. Have fun but keep safe.

This book is dedicated to my sister Natalie who has just started embracing goal setting. If a millennial with over 5,000 unread emails can set goals and not feel overwhelmed by it, then anyone can.

CONTENTS

Reader Gift: The Happy20 ix
1. What Are You Waiting For? 1
2. Is Super Sexy Goal Setting For You? 7
3. Goal Setting Objections 15
4. The F Word 25
5. Why Super Sexy Goal Setting Works 33
6. Five Benefits Of Super Sexy Goal Setting 39
7. Write Your Goals Wish List 45
8. Write Your Four Super Sexy Goals 53
9. Take Action (Eat Elephants And Frogs) 61
10. Goal Setting Problems And Solutions 71
11. Supercharge Your Super Sexy Goals 79
12. The Real Goal Of This Book 91

Reader Gift: The Happy20 95
About the Author 97
Books by Julie Schooler 99
Acknowledgments 101
Please Leave a Review 103
References 105

READER GIFT: THE HAPPY20

There is no doubt that having goals will transform your life, but it is also important to remember to squeeze the best out every single day. To remind you of this, I created

THE HAPPY20
20 Free Ways to Boost Happiness in 20 Seconds or Less

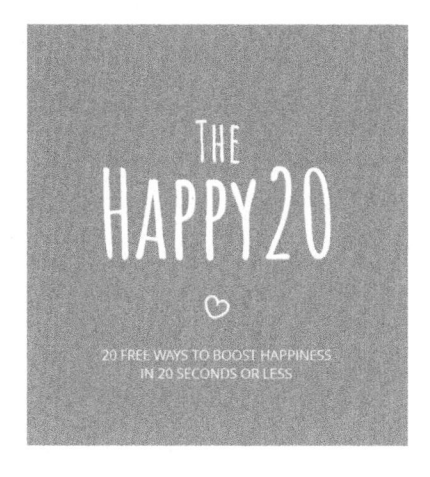

A PDF gift for you with quick ideas to improve mood and add a little sparkle to your day.

Head to **JulieSchooler.com/gift** and grab your copy today.

1

WHAT ARE YOU WAITING FOR?

> 'Life is what happens to you when you are busy making other plans.' – John Lennon

Is This You?

- Have your previous attempts at setting goals been too difficult or overwhelming?
- Are you sick of failed goals and New Year's resolutions that go nowhere?
- Does the thought of goal setting seem so serious and boring it puts you off even attempting it?

We are promised that goal setting is an amazing way to transform our lives for the better, but it just seems like a hard chore that can often end in spectacular failure.

You may have given up on setting goals because it is frustrating and you haven't seen the results you want. Or perhaps you have never tried to set goals because the whole thing seems to take way too long and may not work, anyway.

Maybe you have spent too long working on other people's agendas and spending time and energy doing what you don't want, it is hard to even imagine focusing on what you do want and taking steps to achieve it.

But deep down you know that there is a power to setting goals. On the rare occasions you have stuck to a goal, you have felt a degree of success. You just want to find a way to set goals that excites you, a way that keeps you taking action and that enhances your life without adding to your never-ending to-do list. However, you are so busy you don't even know where to start.

You want to set goals that you KNOW will work and that will also not suck the last tiny bit of spare time and enjoyment out of your life.

Bringing Sexy Back

This book will provide you with the simplest and most fun way to set goals that will radically overhaul your life in just one year. Instead of adding to your workload, narrowing the focus to just FOUR 'super sexy' goals will remove inessential busyness and return your daily life to focusing on what is vitally important to you.

As one of the goals will focus on having fun in any way you want to think about it—relaxing on the beach with a loved one, doing a backyard waterslide with the kids or checking off some places on your travel bucket list—you will always have an element of fun as part of your four super sexy goals.

This easy-to-read guide will also cut through the confusion around how to set goals that are simple to remember and perfect for you, provide compelling reasons why super sexy goals are an essential part of life and tell you exactly what to do to work them out—even if you have never set goals before.

In less than a couple of hours this book will give you the exact blueprint to writing your own super sexy goals that span the next 12 months. You won't need to spend hours searching for information all over the Internet. You will have a clear direction and won't be confused by conflicting advice. Your new, super sexy list of only FOUR goals will help you spring out of bed every morning with renewed enthusiasm for living, not just existing.

For the first time ever, you will achieve your New Year's resolutions.

If It Works for Me...

I have set goals every year for over ten years and can see the immense power in them—if they are written and acted upon in the right way. Purely through goal setting I have achieved things I never thought possible, like running a half-marathon (even though I hated running), completing 40 bucket list items in one year and writing five books.

People ask me all the time how I am able to achieve so much. The formula is simple but extremely powerful: I set a handful of exciting, emotionally charged and meaningful goals for the year ahead. These are the super sexy goals that I want more than anything else in the next 12 months. Then I create absolute conviction around the fact that I will achieve them. I make sure I have the resources to tackle any obstacles that arise and the right mindset to face my fears. Finally, I make sure my life is ordered so I can schedule the goal tasks in and give them the focus they deserve.

I realized that I could not find one short, clear, entertaining guide on how to set and get goals this way. So I distilled the avalanche of information, and all my learnings from years of goal setting, into simple and practical tips to help you write your super sexy goals and then take action.

You gain my best insights to overcome challenges and avoid common mistakes. This book contains all the tools, advice and inspiration you need to make this your best year ever with goals that will make your heart sing.

I have written the book that I wanted to read.

Benefits

Just think how great it will be when you have your own super sexy goals list. There are benefits in so many areas. You will:

- rediscover buried dreams and understand your true self better
- know exactly how to determine what you want in life, not what you don't want
- feel good about yourself for following through on goals
- learn and grow by stepping out of your comfort zone
- wake up each morning with a sense of excitement and zest for life
- lead and inspire others to live life on their terms

- feel like you are living the life you were meant to live, one with excitement, meaning and true joy

Applause

Busy people are happy to recommend this book as it contains everything they need and nothing they don't for goal setting. They are excited that there is a finally a short book that helps them to effortlessly write and take action on their most appealing goals for the year. Readers are excited that there is finally a fun and easy-to-read book that removes any stigma that goal setting is boring, difficult or overwhelming.

My Promise to You

This book will make it effortless and exciting to discover your most desirable goals. This is the most fun, stress-free and of course, SEXY book on goal setting you will ever read.

You will write your goals so clearly that you will be able to recite them in your sleep and they will get you bouncing with a joy for life you had forgotten you had.

In addition, I promise that you will have a simple yet robust action plan for completing your top four super sexy goals in the next year.

It is guaranteed that if you use this book to write your goals, you will feel better, this will be your best year ever, and you will give yourself the best gift of all—a feeling of accomplishment in achieving exactly what you want in life.

Don't Be a Statistic

If you don't set goals, someone else will do it for you. You will be adrift on the sea of someone else's plan. I know that is not really what you want, but it has seemed easier up until now.

Do not wait until another year rolls by with failed New Year's resolutions to read this book. Improve your health, relationships and work or business today. Imagine how amazing your life could look in only 12 months time when you achieve your top four super sexy goals.

We often delay really living, but why and for what?

Read this book today and bring some much-needed clarity, direction and joy back into your life.

Live Life By Design

Goal setting need not be boring, complicated or serious. Four super sexy goals. One year. Your life transformed.

This book will reignite that spark you once had. You will learn how to focus on what you really want—to live life by design, not by default.

Ultimately, this book will lead you to be more enriched, fulfilled and motivated, this year and for the rest of your life.

2

IS SUPER SEXY GOAL SETTING FOR YOU?

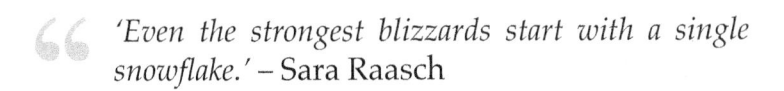

> *'Even the strongest blizzards start with a single snowflake.'* – Sara Raasch

What is Goal Setting?

Here are a few definitions so everyone understands the basics. Then we can move on to the sexy stuff—making your life massively better.

Goal: An outcome or result that a person has committed to achieve in a set timeframe

Goal setting: Working out a plan and action steps to attain a goal

New Year's resolution: Setting a goal (resolution) especially focused on changing or improving an aspect of your life at the start of a new year

Sexy: In this context, sexy means interesting, appealing, attractive or exciting (not the arousing or erotic definition; apologies if this disappoints you!)

Super sexy goal setting: Deciding on and writing down four super sexy goals for the next 12 months and having unwavering dedication and a surefire action plan to achieve them

Goal setting, in a traditional sense, may be thought of as hard, serious and prone to failure. Super sexy goal setting is easy, fun and guaranteed to work if you commit to it.

Who is this Book For?

This book is for anyone from 9 to 90 who wants to live a more fulfilling and fun life by setting goals and taking action to achieve them. If you can check those rather large boxes, then this book is for you.

Super sexy goal setting is NOT for you if you want your life to stay exactly the same. It is NOT for you if you wish your life to get better but you can't really commit to doing anything to change it. And it is NOT for you if you are not willing to write your goals down.

This book is especially NOT for you if you are content with being average. The average person in the Western world is broke and unhappy. Don't believe me? A survey from 2015 found that over 40% of US households had less than $2,000 in savings. Over a third of Americans have saved absolutely nothing for retirement. Over 300 million people globally suffer from depression—and that is just the reported statistics! Despite anti-depression drugs not working in a third of cases, anti-depressant use has increased over 60% in the past decade. The World Health Organization has singled out depression as the leading cause of disability globally, beating out cancer and heart disease combined.

Oh, and this book is NOT for you if you don't like straight up talk and hard truths.

Super sexy goal setting is the most fun you will ever have setting goals, but there is still work to do. You must be prepared to figure out and write down four goals. And you need to have the commitment to take some action to achieve them or at least make inroads on them in the next 12 months. Note that this can be any 12-month period and you do not have to wait for the start of a new year.

Do not worry if you have no idea what you really want and cannot even imagine how to take action in your already cluttered schedule. As long as you have a desire to change or improve your life and to give goal setting a good try, this book will take care of the rest.

It is also advantageous if you keep an open mind about new concepts and trying things out. This means that sometimes you will fail at things, and sometimes things won't happen as you would like, and you will have to learn to deal with that. Why not test whether affirmations help you with your goals or practice politely saying 'No' so you can focus on what is really important? If an idea in this book resonates, then try it, but if it doesn't, then try something else. There is a truckload of helpful tips in here —pick your favorites and see what works for your situation.

Why I Wrote This Book

Less than 10% of people set written, positive goals each year.

Less than 10%!

I wrote this book to inspire more people to write goals. My ultimate vision is a world in which 100% of us embrace goal setting, make positive changes in our lives and experience first hand the power that goals can have in creating a fulfilling life.

Imagine the kind of world we would live in if we even doubled or tripled the current number of people who have goals. I would take an educated guess that the levels of broke and unhappy people would decrease significantly. The world would be a very different place.

This book is here to help you focus on what you really want. The average person is thinking about what they don't want. More on why this is soon. If you get nothing else out of this book except for a mindset shift that leans more towards what you want out of your life than what you don't want, then writing this book has been worth it.

People have all sorts of excuses about why they don't set goals, but if one of those reasons is that goal setting seems extraordinarily boring, then you have come to the right place. Believe me, I have read many goal setting books that are so dull and serious they almost turned me off goal setting. Me! The person who wants the entire population of the globe to adopt a goal-setting revolution!

The last reason I wrote this book is to bring a whole gigantic bouncy castle of FUN back into goal setting. We all need fun in our lives but tend to dismiss it as childish or selfish. It is neither. Instead of childish, fun is a vital element to achievement—it is much easier to achieve things with a sprinkle of joy added in. And it is definitely not selfish. If we invite grace and light into our lives, people around us will, too.

I wrote this book to inspire more people to rediscover their true desires, set goals and add a bit of fun back into their lives. Doesn't that sound sexy?

THE HALF MARATHON

The power of goal setting is best illustrated in a story from my own life.

A few years ago, I attended a motivational seminar that included a 'fire walking experience'. I had no intention of doing the fire walk, but the rest of the seminar sounded interesting so I signed up. I did end up doing the fire walk and it didn't hurt a bit. Don't ask me to explain why. All I can tell you is the feeling I got afterwards. I felt incredible. Here was something I never imagined I could do, and I did it. I walked on fire! I was invincible! I could do anything! (Big disclaimer—please do not attempt a fire walk without the proper guidance and professional oversight.)

Right after the fire walk I decided to run the Auckland half marathon, a distance of 21km or 13 miles. I had not run since I was a kid over 20 years back, and never at that distance. I had decided when I was young that I hated running and I believed it would damage my feet. So this goal was a definite challenge for me! And it didn't stop there—I had a number of obstacles to face.

The first obstacle I came up against was money. I bought the half marathon ticket. I bought new running shoes. I bought a few pairs of specially designed running socks at $30 each—$30 just for one pair of socks! I went to a podiatrist and got his opinion and bought orthotics for my new gym shoes. I ended up spending $700 before I took a single running step.

And that wasn't even the hard work—then I started running! The Auckland half marathon is something special as it gives you the chance to go on foot over the Harbor Bridge, which is vehicle only. That bridge is steep! I heard that if you didn't make it over the Harbor Bridge in a set time period a bus picked you up—and this "bus of shame" story kept me motivated to run up a lot of hills.

If someone had told me about all the things I would have to do and what I would go through before I crossed that finish line, I would have given up. But I had an absolute determination about completing the half marathon. I just knocked each obstacle out of the way—money, training, pain—it didn't matter.

One of the reasons I had such determination is that I painted a picture describing exactly what I would be doing when I achieved my goal. In this case:

> 'I have just completed the Auckland half marathon in less than 2 ½ hours and I am feeling great and my support team is patting me on the back and telling me well done'.

Completing the half marathon and doing it within 2 ½ hours—I could do that. But the really funny thing is, I was reading my goal every day before the run and I hadn't actually done anything about the support crew. As the half marathon started very early in the morning I had organized for my boyfriend to drop me at the start line and then I was to call him when I got to the end to pick me up. I was running by myself and no one was going to meet me at the finish line.

Well, as I turned the corner and ran the last part towards the finish line, I heard my name being called—"Julie, Julie". I looked over to where all the people were crowded watching the runners and there was my Dad and my sister, Natalie, and a couple of friends, all waving and cheering me on.

I got to the finish line and they all came and found me straight away, giving me hugs, patting my back, shaking my hand and telling me well done.

In short, even though I didn't plan or force it that way, my goal happened EXACTLY how I wrote it down.

Be Exceptional

I want more people to experience the pure magic of the decisive focus, conviction and vividly described goals that form super sexy goal setting. You will feel a major sense of achievement in setting and achieving four goals in one year. And you will grow as a person as you step out of your comfort zone and create memories out of your dreams. I don't want you to be average. I want you to be exceptional.

> This is a short book but—and this is not said lightly
> —it WILL change your life.

If you are a 'get to the point' person, then feel free to skip the next few chapters and go straight to Chapter Seven.

From that point on are all the strategies you need to decide on your four super sexy goals and start taking action on them. However, mindset is a major part of the success of goal setting, so if you need a bit more convincing that this is for you, keep reading right through.

3

GOAL SETTING OBJECTIONS

> *'If you are interested, you will do what is convenient; if you are committed, you will do whatever it takes.'* – John Assaraf

Reasons versus Excuses

So why do you not have goals right now, or why are you not following through on goals you have made? There are plenty of seemingly valid reasons not to have goals or to let them fall away into oblivion.

It is important to review the main goal-setting objections well, objectively. The next chapter will dive into the underlying reasons why we voice these excuses in the first place (hint: it is a four-letter word starting with F). For now, let's bust apart these stories.

'Goal setting seems way too complicated'

Goal setting looks like a lot of hard work, you don't know where to start and it may not even work, so why bother? On the surface, this really does look like a valid reason. Just a quick delve into goals and goal-setting literature brings up more questions than answers. For example:

- Don't I have to have a life plan in place and know my purpose before writing my goals?
- Should I write small, achievable goals to make me feel like a success or big, hairy audacious goals ('BHAGs') to stretch myself?
- Are goals the same as desires, dreams, wishes or wants?
- Do I focus on the end goal or what I will learn along the way?
- How are habits, routines, systems and resolutions tied in with goals?
- What areas of my life should I cover when setting goals?
- How many goals should I write in total and for each area of my life?
- Should I be writing goals out for the next week, month, year, five years, ten years, the whole rest of my life?
- Is it a good idea to map out all action steps and have a plan with the goal?

No wonder less than 10% of the population writes goals. With that list of bewilderment and confusion, I am surprised even small percentages embark on goal setting.

Forget about the answers to the questions above. With super sexy goal setting, you will be focusing on four challenging yet achievable goals for one year. You will be shown the very best way to write them so you are excited about them. You will get tips on how to put them into action and keep the momentum going. Super sexy goals strip away the extra stuff and only focus on what is most important and what works.

'I AM WAY TOO BUSY AND DON'T HAVE TIME FOR GOALS'

Having goals may seem like a good idea, but on top of a busy life, adding goals to the mix seems like an impossible ask. You may have work, kids, a partner, a household to run. You have a big full life. If you can't spend three minutes in the bathroom in peace, writing out goals and taking action on them is just crazy talk.

Being busy is a competitive sport these days, and everyone looks like they are striving for the gold medal for 'busy champion of the world'. Are you really so busy you cannot spend some time on what is most important to you? Many people mistake movement for achievement. Everyone has the same number of hours in the day, but the successful few prioritize what is really essential and delegate or eliminate the rest.

The truth is that selecting well-written and clear goals will actually cut the busyness and overwhelm out of your life. You NEED goals to gain clarity and rid yourself of the busy parts that add nothing to your life. Right now, you may not think anything can be removed from your life to make way for goals, but if you find the right goals to focus and work on, other parts of your life will shift to accommodate what is truly important to you.

You will write four goals. These are the four most crucial things to focus on for the next 12 months. If something comes up, ask yourself, "Is this thing more important than my top four goals?"

> The vital part to remember is that goals will reduce, not increase, what you really need to do.

Be honest with yourself and don't say you don't have time. Admit that you don't have priorities. Acknowledge that you don't have clarity. Concede that not making decisions about what is really important is a way to absolve yourself from determining your destiny.

'Don't I have to know my life's purpose first?'

If you do have a purpose already, great, but it is NOT a prerequisite for choosing goals. You don't need to work out your whole life plan or your vision or mission statement or what you want your legacy to be. Phew! What a relief that all that serious navel gazing work can be jettisoned.

To flip this thought around, goal setting can help determine a more purposeful direction in life. You often don't know what your passions are until you work on them. The occasional few laps in the pool and bike to work becomes triathlon training. Writing in your journal each morning starts your memoir. Salsa dancing lessons with your partner take you to a regional competition.

At the very least, taking action on your goals helps you acquire skills that may come in handy later when you have figured it all out. Steve Jobs took a calligraphy class at college that later in his life had a major influence on the design of Apple products. He could never have known that taking one random college class would have had an impact on the typography of personal computers all over the world.

'I SET GOALS IN THE PAST AND IT DIDN'T WORK OUT'

Do you give up on other things in your life or decide not to commit anymore, as you 'know' it won't work? How is that working out for you?

Failure is a big reason why people do not set goals, and this will be explored more in the next chapter. The main question to answer here is WHY you failed at your goals. There are so many reasons for a goals failure that you can't just dismiss all goals for the rest of time as 'bad'. Instead, delve into why the goal didn't work so you can rectify a specific weak spot.

Perhaps the goals were not written properly, or at all, usually in the case of New Year's resolutions. Maybe they were not exciting or compelling enough to keep your interest up. Perhaps there wasn't enough structure in place—scheduling or deadlines—to carry on with them. Maybe you wrote too many or they were in conflict. Competing goals will be explored in Chapter Ten—this can be a major reason why goals don't work. Examining exactly why your goals failed can tell you what to do differently next time.

And there will be a next time. With these four super sexy goals, there will be minimal chance that you will lose interest, won't schedule them in or have a conflict so you will be more likely to continue with your goals.

· · ·

'I am worried about what others might think'

If you set goals and publicly announce them, then you have some accountability, which is a good way to stay on track. However, this can have the reverse effect: if for some reason you don't achieve your goal or it is a goal that people don't like, then you face public scrutiny.

First, you don't have to tell everyone about your goals. If you really think it is a good way to stay accountable and the downside of possible negative judgment doesn't bother you, then by all means splash your goals all over social media. But if you think that it will actually decrease your motivation, then keep your goals to yourself or only tell a couple of close friends who will be cheerleaders for you no matter what.

Second, who cares what people think? Unless they are paying your electricity bill, they have no say in your life. Remember most people don't set goals and most people end up broke and unhappy, so do you really want to take on opinions from the average person?

And last, most people don't care or notice, anyway. They are not judging you. They are competing for 'busy champion of the world' or staring at their phones. People only really care if it affects them, and what you are doing probably doesn't.

'I am not the goal setting type'

You have decided you are not the type of person who has goals. Goal setting doesn't suit your personality or the way you live your life. Deciding that 'I am' something that is contradictory to being a goal setter is a great story to tell yourself to get out of it. It is so believable as you have tied your identity to not liking goal setting. Once you put 'I am' in front of something, it seems like a fixed truth even though it is simply a limiting belief.

You may say positive things about yourself that imply having goals is bad. For instance, 'I am spontaneous' or 'I am fun loving' or 'I live in the present and am not ambitious'. But people who set goals don't think of themselves as rigid, dull or ruthless. Instead they think goals give them more chance of an exciting life, of reaching their potential and adding value into the world. How you frame yourself against your belief about goals makes a big difference.

Strangely, you can even paint yourself in a negative light to get out of writing goals. 'I am a procrastinator' is a primary example. You are not a procrastinator! You may sometimes procrastinate if you don't like what you are doing or are feeling tired or are scared of the next step, but it is an outside factor. It is not you. If someone put a gun to your head and said you had to get X done, you wouldn't tell them 'But I am a procrastinator'. You would do it. Immediately.

'MY LIFE IS PRETTY GOOD SO WHY STRIVE FOR MORE?'

This little gem of an untruthful 'truth' crops up in different ways. In the excuses that 'My kids need me' or 'I will wait until the kids are older'. Or perhaps a guilt trip notion of 'I have enough already' or 'Who am I to ask for more when I have so much?'

Your kids need role models to show them that goals can be set and achieved. They need to see someone striving to be their very best. They need to be shown first hand how to fail well—pick themselves up, dust themselves off and keep going. They NEED you to set goals.

You owe it to the world to use up every single tiny ounce of all the resources and riches that you were so fortunately bestowed with to reach your potential, create value and share your gifts with the world. It would be a travesty if you just settled because you thought you didn't deserve even more from life.

And are you really happy in every area of your life? Probably not. We tell ourselves we love our comfort zones because outside of them is a scary place. More on comfort zones in the next chapter. But for now, be honest with yourself. Are you dissatisfied in some areas of your life? Good! Get excited, as now you may be willing to take action.

'I am too…'

There are tons of other reasons why people decide to not set goals, and this would be a very long chapter if I itemized each one.

Too tired? Goals actually give you a renewed sense of purpose that helps you spring out of bed in the morning. Not only will prioritizing what you want and focusing on the most important goals give you clarity but also more energy.

Too expensive? Well some can be. Space shuttle flights are still a tad pricey. So choose goals that don't cost a lot or that can actually save you money. Learning to cook a great meal, writing a book or going for a swim all cost pennies and actually help you become healthier and happier.

You are not too old. You are not too young. You are not too uneducated or too poor, and you are not too busy. You are not too purple or too green or any other 'too' you tell yourself you are. You are not too late. Too late only applies when the zombie apocalypse happens, not before.

The last chapter gave you a taster of how frank I can be, but think of this book as more of an honest coach to you than a sympathetic friend. Your objections to goals and goal setting are just excuses so you can feel okay about your average life. They help you justify why you are not trying to reach your full potential. They are stories you tell to yourself that make it tolerable that you are not taking action on your dreams. They help you feel good about settling for mediocrity.

Choose Your Hard

Overall, many of the objections we have stem from an inherent conflict where we want to be content with our present lives while also wanting a better future. For instance, we want to treat our bodies with respect and kindness but also acknowledge we want to tone up and lose a little weight. It is hard to juggle this paradox. But just because it is hard doesn't meant that goal setting is wrong. It is natural to want more.

> The key to a successful life is to appreciate where
> we currently are but still constantly improve,
> dream and plan.

This will be said a few times throughout the book: getting your head around this present versus future conflict is hard. Not doing anything with your life because you are using a silly paradox or some other thing as an excuse is also hard. <u>Choose your hard.</u>

These objections all have the same underlying cause. Let us delve into the real reason for all this anti-goal-setting sentiment in the next chapter.

4
THE F WORD

> *'Avoiding danger is no safer in the long run than outright exposure. The fearful are caught as often as the bold.'* – Helen Keller

The Real Reason

We were able to smash though all those seemingly valid reasons to avoid goal setting in the previous chapter with a bit of logic and common sense, so why do we offer up so many objections against goals? There has to be something underlying the myriad excuses.

That something is, of course... drum roll please... dah, dah, de, dah... FEAR. We don't set goals, we give up on goals and we don't take action on goals because we are afraid.

There are a number of reasons why we are scared of setting goals, including being worried about rejection, disapproval, making the wrong decision or missing out on something else. Even success and accomplishment can make people scared. If you stand out, you can be knocked down. Or you don't want to start something in case you achieve a goal and it does not make you as happy or successful as you expected.

The biggest fear for the vast majority is a fear of failure. Let us take a closer look at failure and hopefully get a new perspective on it.

Failure

Understandably, goal setting is associated with a fear of failure. You may set a goal that does not work out. This can mean a loss of time that could have been spent on something else, a loss of money, even a loss of something bigger—a house, a business, friends, your reputation in the community. Of course you fear failure if you associate it with loss in this way, but there are ways to look at failure that don't have such serious implications.

First, be sensible with your goal setting by making sure you don't set goals that have more than a tiny chance of catastrophic loss. If you want to start a new business, don't quit your job and mortgage your house up to the hilt. Start slowly, on the side. Dream big and also plan your goals to minimize the downside.

Second, know that you will fail. Oh you will fail. Sometimes you will fall down so spectacularly and so hard that you are not sure if your tailbone will ever feel right again. But you will also learn to get back up, dust yourself off and keep going. Whether that means overcoming an obstacle to get to the goal, or making a decision to veer onto another goal, your true character is built not on whether you fail but on how and when you pick yourself back up again. Maybe next time you will fail better! Failure is part of goal setting—you need to find a way to be okay with that.

Third, the thought of failure shouldn't stop you from trying. Perhaps you only write half a book by the deadline, or only make a few dollars in your side business or cross the finish line after everyone else has gone home. So what? You did better than everyone who never tried. You can do it again and do it better. You learned a lot, gained skills, and now you know what to focus on to improve next time.

> If you shoot for the stars and only land on the moon, you can still be proud of what you achieved.

Last, know that all the most successful people have failed. Failed big time. Failure means that you are playing this game called life, not sitting on the sidelines. This list may help you feel better about any failures that happen to you in your goal-setting journey:

- Oprah Winfrey was fired from her first TV job at a local news station as she was 'unfit for television'.
- J.K. Rowling's *Harry Potter* manuscript was rejected by all 12 major publishers.
- Elvis Presley failed an audition to become part of a vocalist quartet as he was told he 'couldn't sing'.
- Walt Disney was fired from his newspaper job because he 'lacked imagination and had no good ideas'.
- George Lucas' script for *Star Wars* was turned down by two major film studios, and 20th Century Fox only took it on because of his exemplary reputation even though they didn't understand it.

- Michael Jordan, at 15, was passed up for his high school basketball team.

Jordan is credited with saying that, "I've missed more than 9,000 shots in my career. I've lost almost 300 games. And 26 times, I've been trusted to take the game winning shot and missed. I've failed over and over and over again in my life. And that is why I succeed."

THREE LEVELS OF FEAR

Susan Jeffers says in her classic personal development book, *Feel the Fear and do it Anyway*, that fear has three levels:

1. Surface story: These are the excuses and objections we discussed in the previous chapter—the 'I am too busy / tired / old' story.
2. Inner states of mind: This is the fear of failure, success, rejection, disapproval or missing out, etc., described above.
3. I Can't Handle It!: At the bottom of every one of your fears is simply the fear that you cannot handle whatever life may bring you.

The real reason you do not set goals is because you do not think you can handle what life brings you as a result of setting the goal. This may be the thought that you won't be able to tackle the obstacles that arise, or you won't be able to deal with the outcome of the goal itself. Why do you think, 'I Can't Handle It'? Where does this underlying fear come from?

It comes from The Lizard.

• • •

The Lizard

Not a pet lizard, but The Lizard that resides in your brain. You are evolutionarily hardwired for survival. In prehistoric times, humans needed a robust flight-or-fight-or-freeze mechanism for when we spotted a sabre tooth tiger, or when it spotted us. In your head right this very moment is a little area near the brain stem called the amygdala, and it prompts you to constantly scan for anything that can kill you.

As this is a survival tool from a primitive era, the author, coach, and wise soul, Martha Beck, describes this part of you as 'The Lizard'. The Lizard is a reptilian animal in your brain that perks its head up and alerts you to anything you perceive as scary or scarce. It does this to protect you, but it means your brain is wired to find the negative at all times.

The Lizard tells you things are scary even if they are not. It alters your perception. In the Western world, you live in one of the most abundant and safe times in human history. As there is nothing really dangerous going on, The Lizard turns its attention to other things it thinks you might like to worry about.

Your Lizard now tells you day in and day out that you lack time, energy, money or love. Think about that for a moment: instead of being scarce in water, food or shelter, your Lizard brain is trying to protect you by telling you that time, energy, money or love are scarce and need to be conserved. It is fake fear, but it feels very real.

Due to your Lizard fear you now don't want to do anything to jeopardize all the existing time, energy, money or love you currently have. Even if you are dissatisfied with your life, your Lizard tells you not to try and strive for more in case you lose it all. Because if you lose it all, it says you can't handle it.

The Comfort Zone

What your Lizard and its accompanying fear of 'I can't handle it' do is keep you in your comfort zone. People think they don't want to leave their comfort zones, as it feels pleasant and familiar, and they feel safe and in control of their environments. Going to work, coming back to your home, watching TV, these are all nice at times. Being in your comfort zone is comfortable, but after a while it actually starts to hurt you. You start to feel unenthused and jaded with your routine existence.

Stepping out of your comfort zone and trying new things leads to growth, and growth is necessary for a fulfilling life. Successful people are prepared to step outside their comfort zones. The real magic happens there, so even if it feels uneasy at first, you must try to counter the Lizard and your fears and go for your goals.

Most people do not realize they live pretty crappy lives by not really trying to accomplish what they can and to realize their potential.

Dance with the Fear

Your Lizard and its 'I can't handle it' fear signal has been a driving force that has kept you in your comfort zone. Then your mind has made up stories to make you feel better about playing small in the one life you are gifted with.

But please, please, please don't beat yourself up about this. Do something with this newfound wisdom instead.

The paradoxical truth about fear is that it will never go away unless you go out and do the thing you fear. The only way to blast away the fear is to take action. Set goals, learn, grow. Don't fight the fear or hide from it, dance with fear instead.

The past two chapters have conquered your objections to goal setting and explained that the best way to overcome your fears is to take action on your goals. The next two chapters will explain what the super sexy goal system is, why it will work for you and all its super sexy benefits.

5

WHY SUPER SEXY GOAL SETTING WORKS

> *'Motivation is what gets you started. Habit is what keeps you going.'* – Jim Rohn

SUPER SEXY GOAL SETTING OVERVIEW

Super sexy goal setting is deciding on and writing down four super sexy goals for the next 12 months and having unwavering dedication and a surefire action plan to achieve them.

WHY 12 MONTHS?

Choosing goals that take a year allows a clear deadline to be in place but also provides enough time to complete something challenging. Both these factors make you feel like you have accomplished something worthwhile.

This can be any 12-month period. You don't have to start at the beginning of the calendar year. Start now! Also, you can do all four goals over the entire 12-month period or focus on particular goals in certain periods within the year, say one each quarter. Think ONE YEAR. No more than that.

Why four goals?

You will get more done by doing less. Focusing on four goals keeps your finite amounts of attention, time and resources narrowed on the most important areas of your life that you want to improve. There are a lot of good things to do, but narrowing down to four makes you focus only on the great things. As author Jim Collins argues: "good is the enemy of the great". Remember you only have 12 months. You can do another four next year! Think FOUR GOALS. No more than that.

What areas should the goals cover?

You can choose any area of your life in which to set goals. Start with the part of your life with which you are most dissatisfied. If you want to follow the exact system in this book, then choose one goal for each of the three main areas of your life—health, relationships and work/business. The fourth area is called 'just for you'—something fun or a hobby or a skill to master or an exciting challenge. Think FOUR AREAS. No more than that.

Why It Works

The reason super sexy goal setting is different from other goal-setting strategies is that it makes goals exciting, easy to action and emotionally fulfilling. It compels you to actually want to set goals and achieve them.

It does this by weaving some of the core principles from psychology and personal development into its system. These then allow you to rediscover your power to create the life you truly desire. Let's take a brief look at these concepts.

Pain and Pleasure

No matter what stories you tell yourself, the only reason you don't have goals is that you have linked more pain or less pleasure to having the goal than to not having it. Your equation up until now is goal equals pain or no goal equals pleasure.

Pain and pleasure are the major drivers of animal behavior. Everything we do in life is driven by our need to avoid pain or gain pleasure. We think we are complex beings, humans with imagination and emotion and conscious decision-making abilities, but when it comes down to it we are just like Pavlov's dogs.

Think about it: why did that New Year's Resolution to go for a run every morning fail? Because getting out of your cozy bed in the dark and cold seems more painful than hitting the snooze button. Why did you give up on writing that book? Because the latest binge-watching sensation seemed much more enjoyable than wrestling with words on a blank document.

The key to an outstanding life is utilizing these unavoidable drivers to our advantage. Link extraordinary amounts of pleasure to taking action on goals and not attempting a goal to massive, immediate pain. Switch around the equation. Goal equals pleasure. No goal equals pain.

The way the super sexy goal system works is to link huge amounts of pleasure to your goals. There are only four goals, there is a relatively short time frame, they are written in the most desirable way and one of the goals is an exciting or fun challenge just for you, so there is a lot of enjoyment woven in. Not getting the goal automatically starts to feel immensely painful.

Willpower and Momentum

People think they need a whole truckload of willpower to accomplish goals. Thank goodness that this is incorrect as willpower is a fickle beast. It gets used up especially fast on those crazy days when your youngest vomits all over the carpet and you have a flat tire.

You only need a pinch of willpower to start creating some momentum. Once you have momentum there is no stopping you. You need to nudge the boulder off its ledge, and then it will start to tumble down the hill on its own. So how do you kick start willpower? There are only two ways to start to do something. Either you are pushed into it or pulled into it.

If you are pushed you are told to do it, or you are paid to do it, or you are cajoled somehow, say with bribes or rewards. No one likes this sleazy salesman approach much, but with goals, 'push motivation' is helpful to get you through a hard patch. Can't seem to start a new exercise routine? Booking a non-refundable personal training session will get you to the gym. Don't want to finish writing that next chapter? A reward of chocolate or TV could help.

Ultimately what you want is an abundance of 'pull motivation'. You want to want it. You don't want to reluctantly fork out money to the sleazy salesman. You want to happily hand over your credit card. With goals, pull motivation means you go to the gym and work out hard because you enjoy the strength and energy you gain from it. It means you write the next chapter because you are excited to see the characters come alive on the page or you can't wait to share the story with the world. Look, this won't happen all the time with all your goals, but when it does it is magical. Knowing it can happen is a good start.

Super sexy goal setting takes into account both push and pull motivations to create momentum, rather than relying on willpower. Push motivations such as deadlines, accountability and rewards are all optional parts of the system. In addition, pull motivation is linked to every aspect of the goals strategy. It is included in the positive way they are written right through to tools to help you feel great on the journey to achieving your goals.

What Successful People Do

The real reason goals fail is that you don't take enough account of underlying beliefs and emotions. You only do something because of how you think it will make you feel. The average person feels fearful of goals and associates them with pain. The successful person dances with the fear and links goals to pleasure, no matter what.

Turning tasks that are good for you but you initially dislike into pleasurable experiences is the secret to a meaningful and fulfilling life. The most successful people do the things that the average person won't do. They make a habit of being uncomfortable.

For goals this means you must find a way to change your belief to add joy to something that might not initially be thought of as easy or fun. Whether you use rewards or find ways to inherently love the journey, you must make the next action taken on a goal as enjoyable as possible.

> The key to successfully completing goals is converting tasks that you may not like but are good for you into positive experiences that you want to do.

The good news is that this principle is woven into the fabric of the super sexy goal system. You don't have to worry about how you will dramatically transform your beliefs overnight. Just follow the system and they will naturally be revolutionized.

This chapter told you exactly what the super sexy goal-setting system is and gave you a peek behind the curtain of why it is so powerful. Let us look at some benefits of super sexy goals to finish off this mindset part of the book so we can get you juiced up to take action on writing your goals.

6

FIVE BENEFITS OF SUPER SEXY GOAL SETTING

> *'It's about being alive and feisty and not sitting down and shutting up even though people would like you to.'* – P!nk, singer

1. A Little Bit Naughty

You can't have *Super Sexy Goal Setting* as a title of a book without the whole thing feeling a little bit naughty. I want you to dismiss the notion that goals are for boring, organized, responsible people. I want you to take that idea out of your head.

Finding goals that challenge you as a person, that help you grow and allow you to focus on what is really important, is an ultimate rebellion against the system.

Goal setting is an act of defiance to a culture that wants you to be continuously distracted, overwhelmed with day-to-day priorities and focused on the next material purchase to make you feel good. Super sexy goal setting is a way to make you feel more alive and in control of the one life you have.

> Be a rebel. Set some goals.

Here are four other benefits of super sexy goal setting.

2. You Don't Have to Know Your Purpose

You don't need to work out your purpose in life to decide on four goals for the next 12 months. If you do already know it, great, use it to give you some direction in choosing your goals. But it is not a mandatory part of the goal-setting process.

If you decide that you need to know your purpose before you embark on goals, then you make goal setting needlessly complicated, it takes a lot more time, and in the way of all good procrastination attempts, it may stop you from setting any goals at all.

Of course finding your purpose in life is so important that I will be writing a book on it, but for the moment, let us jump in the deep end. Set some goals, achieve some goals, see that the process works, get momentum and take action on more goals. This is more important than navel gazing right now.

The really great thing about choosing four goals and having a short time span in which to achieve them is that taking action on the goals makes you much more likely to work out direction and meaning for your life. Instead of thinking purpose comes before action, action can actually precede purpose. How can you know your entire life's purpose until you try something and see if you can stick to it for 12 months?

Linking everything to a life's purpose sounds so heavy. Instead, with super sexy goal setting you take a lighter approach: pick a direction, start down that path and see if you like it. If you like it, continue: create a positive habit, master a skill, grow as a person. And if you don't, you have gained valuable feedback about what your life's purpose is not going to be about.

3. Incorporating Goals Leads to LESS Overwhelm

You would think that if you add four goals into an already hectic life, you are going to stress yourself out. But the opposite is true.

These goals help you focus on what is really important in your life. As they are the most important things, other things have to take a back seat or be eliminated altogether. Yes, you still have to pick your kids up from school, do your tax returns and floss, but a lot of the superfluous extra busyness will fall way when you build up your prioritizing muscle. You won't feel the need to mindlessly swipe a screen or get caught up in the next binge watch sensation—you have more important things to do.

The fact that you are taking on no more than four goals for one year means you can be concrete about exactly what you need to get done. You are not thinking abstractly way into the future. In addition, this book gives you tools, such as how to reduce decision making in other areas of your life and how to say 'No' politely so you have more time for your goals.

4. It is KISS not SMART

The whole super sexy goal setting system is set up to be as simple as possible because if it is not simple it doesn't get done. Four goals. One year. Written in a way that inspires action and commitment. Achieve more by doing less. That is it.

Goal setting advice makes things needlessly complicated by saying goals should adhere to the 'SMART' acronym. This is my little rant about why SMART is for dummies.

SMART is an acronym that stands for Specific, Measurable, Action, Realistic and Time. Except it doesn't! Sometimes the acronym has Achievable for the A and Relevant for the R. Plus, Time seems to be time-bound, timeframe, time or changed to temporal on occasion. No one agrees on what SMART even stands for, so why are we trying to use that acronym to set our goals?

Moreover, it gives five criteria for setting goals in a kind of abstract way. You have to go back and forth between the specific goal you are trying to write and whether it checks off against each of the criteria (which can't be agreed upon, anyway). By the time you make sure your goal is SMART, you have done so much work you feel like you have achieved your goal when all you have done is achieved the almost impossible task of writing it down 'correctly'.

Lastly, writing a SMART goal, if you are even able to do it, leads to a goal that doesn't have an emotional connection, a vivid portrait of how you will feel and what you will be doing when you get your goal. It is not compelling enough to drive you to take action.

I have an acronym to replace SMART: KISS—keep it simple, stupid.

• • •

5. A Major Focus on Fun

What sets super sexy goal setting apart from the rest is its focus on fun. One goal is just for you. There are no rules here—it is whatever fun looks like to you. It can be exciting (e.g.: travel to exotic places), relaxing (e.g.: reading a novel) or challenging yourself to improve a skill (e.g.: learning a musical instrument).

Why fun at all? Unless we focus on fun, on something we actually enjoy, we will burn out from the other goals and all the other day-to-day activities. This is a positive experience we inherently enjoy, not one we make ourselves like.

Why a goal around fun? One reason is that most people don't emphasize fun in their lives, and it is so important that the only way you may actually do it is to set a goal around doing it. You crave the sweetness of fun at a deep level but disregard it as not important. Then that sweetness you want gets turned into food cravings and before you know it you have devoured an entire block of chocolate. Deciding on fun in a structured way should eliminate it overtaking you in less desirable ways.

The biggest benefit to this fun goal is that you can use it as a reward for completing the other goals with which you may be having a harder time. Yes, you should try and transform experiences you dislike into something more enjoyable, but sometimes things are just hard and the best way to get through them is with some push motivation—bribing or rewarding yourself. So do a hard task and then plan your next vacation or read a few chapters of a novel or strum on your guitar and get the added feeling you are working towards another goal at the same time.

It is a one-two punch of double awesomeness.

Mindset Conclusion

You are half way through the book and you haven't written down a single goal yet. I mean whaaaaat? This first part of the book has been essential to bake in more positive beliefs around goal setting.

You have now learned that no matter what sort of person you are, you can write goals and you will benefit from goal setting. All you need to create things in your life is for your desire to be greater than your fear.

By now you are starting to understand that your emotions, your beliefs and your identity are far more important than willpower, plans and habits. You don't get your goals—you get what you believe you are—your identity.

Sometimes you don't need to learn anything new to achieve real transformation, but instead to UNLEARN what you 'know' or believe. By cracking open those limiting beliefs, you start to rediscover what your heart is telling you to do. Deep down you know what you want; you just have to listen carefully to catch the whispers of your soul.

You have been promised more time, less overwhelm, more fun and less struggle with this super sexy system. If this all seems too good to be true, read on and judge for yourself. The next two chapters will guide you to four written goals that you are genuinely excited about. Let's begin.

7
WRITE YOUR GOALS WISH LIST

> *'If you have a goal, write it down. If you do not write it down, you do not have a goal—you have a wish.'* – Steve Maraboli

Goals Wish List

By the end of this chapter you will have a written list of what you want in life. This is not your final goals list. It is definitely not a to-do list. It is simply a 'goals wish list' to capture your dreams down on paper.

Your list MUST be written down. Writing ideas down makes them real, gets your thoughts in order and is a permanent record of your wants and dreams. Studies have shown that you boost your chances of accomplishing goals by at least 40% if they are written down. A goal that is not in writing is merely a hope or wishful thinking. Writing starts your mind conspiring how the goal could be possible. It creates momentum. Write down your goals wish list!

This may seem simple, but it can be more difficult than you originally thought due to the belief that goal setting must be hard or complicated, your innate ability to focus on what you don't want and how easily distracted humans can be.

You don't have to decide whether this is a 'worthy' goal right now. You don't need to write it in the 'best' way or figure out action steps. And you definitely don't need to think about deadlines or timelines.

Step One: Brainstorm

We are so easily distracted these days, so this will be a timed writing exercise—an hour would be great, but even 20 minutes would be a start. No phones, no Internet.

What you need: something on which to write out your goals wish list—a blank document on your computer, or a large piece of paper or the back of an envelope. Anything will do. Gather up some pens or colored markers as well, if needed. Then find something with which to time yourself—a watch, phone timer or a giant hourglass, for example. Don't do anything else in the time you set aside for this exercise.

Now brainstorm, free write or mind map EVERYTHING you have always wanted to do, see, have, be, meet, etc. You know in your heart what you want.

Have fun with this creative exercise. Be silly, invoke your curiosity, think outside the box. Think about fun things, challenging things, short-term activities, long-term pastimes, local places to visit and trips abroad. Think of your interests, hobbies, and passions. Think of different areas of your life, for instance: health, relationships, work, finances, personal growth, contribution. Dream big. Go wild. Get ridiculous. Get unreasonable. Anything goes. Just write.

Write in short bullet points or long, descriptive paragraphs. Know that anything can be changed or deleted later. Don't worry whether you are describing outcomes or performance-based goals. Don't worry that you don't have time or can't afford it or allow in any other negative thoughts. Don't worry if it seems too exotic or difficult, or conversely, too mundane or easy. If it lights a fire in your belly, then it is perfect. Don't think it is not possible. If someone else in the world has done it, it is possible. Write down what you want in any way that makes sense to you.

Due to your Lizard brain perpetually scanning for danger, you have a bias to pick up negatives much more than positives, so you can often think about what you don't want, rather than what you do want. Use this to your advantage. If you don't like something in your life, or there is something that you can't put up with a moment longer—good! Write that down and then flip it so you can think of a solution. For example, "I don't like the extra pounds I put on" can be flipped to, "I want to lose weight or eat healthier."

If you can't flip, then write down what you don't want. For instance, I don't want to feel this tired, put up with this crappy relationship any longer or be paid so low. This can be a good way to start and will clear the way to what you DO want.

Remember at this point that this does not have to look pretty. It is just a wish list—it will be narrowed down and tidied up later. Writing goals, any goals, is the only important thing.

There is no 'right number' of entries to end on. Just write until you run out of steam or time is up. Then reset your timer and use questions and prompts below to add to and define your wants and dreams even more.

Step Two: Questions and Prompts

Questions and prompts help you to figure out more goals wish list items and also focus on finding items more attuned to you. Using questions has been found to have a massive impact, because if a question is asked, even if it is not spoken aloud, your mind is still compelled to answer it.

There are four general areas of questions. You don't have to answer all these questions. They are just there as prompts so you can add to your goals wish list or to refine it so it reflects YOU.

Santa's Knee Questions

These come in various forms, but overall they help you think like an excited five-year-old sitting on Santa's knee. There are no filters, no limits, no boundaries. Go crazy. Ask for the impossible. For example:

- What would you like if there were no financial limits?
- What would you do if you had unlimited time, money and resources?
- If you won a huge lottery, what would you do?
- If fear were not part of the equation what would you do?
- If you were given three wishes, what would you

wish for (excluding world peace, of course)?

Deathbed Regrets Questions

These help you confront your own mortality. For example:

- What would you like to have said about you in your eulogy?
- What do you absolutely HAVE to do before you die?
- What would be your biggest regret on your deathbed?
- What would you do, see, or have if you only had one year to live?

Passions and Interests Questions

These help you to remember what you have always liked to do, or thought you would be good at but then decided that time, money or something else was in the way. These can be one-off things or longer-term hobbies. For example:

- What was your childhood dream to do, see, create?
- What have you always wanted to do but you felt like you didn't have time?
- What do you want to buy or do just to have fun?
- What would you do even without pay?
- What activity makes you lose track of time?
- What has always been one of your biggest dreams in life?
- What would be a perfect day for you?

Get Down to Specifics Questions

Here are some questions that can help you think about your wish list in alternative ways.

- What would you DO—see or create or accomplish?
- Where would you like to visit or travel—countries, places, locations?
- What new foods do you want to taste?
- Who do you want to meet in person?
- What experiences do you want to have?
- What activities do you want to try at least once?
- What activities or skills do you want to learn or master?
- What adventures would get you out of your comfort zone?
- Are there any special moments or scheduled events you want to witness?

Step Three: Narrow It Down

How good was that!? How do you feel?

You have done something most people never do. The average person spends more time on working out what is for dinner than what he wants out of life.

Now I want you to pick FOUR goals that you can focus on for the next 12 months and discard the rest.

Whaaaaat!?

Don't throw them away completely—keep your wish list somewhere you can find it again. But after you have chosen your four goals, don't refer to it for 12 months.

Yikes!

This may be such a hard ask that it makes you want to stop the goal setting altogether. Please don't do that, you have come this far and now you just need to make a decision or two.

We live in a world where we can do anything, but prioritizing what is really important is an essential skill. It is easier than ever in this day and age to get ideas, but it's also easy to be overwhelmed, have your focus split and then get burned out. You need to narrow down to four super sexy goals. I know you like many of these goals, but remember good is the enemy of the great.

The first way to decide on four goals is to go through your list and find the ones that jump out at you, that your gut instinct tells you would be amazing to do, that really excite you. If you are not really excited, then why is it a goal? Circle those.

Next, get a bit practical and decide what you could actually do in the next 12 months. This should only take out the very long-term goals—perhaps building your dream home or flying to the moon—but you could create a one-year goal around getting to the larger goals. Circle the ones that fit.

Last, if you want to keep your goals balanced across your life, then find one goal in each of the main categories: health, relationships and work/business, plus one fun or challenge goal just for you. Circle the best goals out of those categories.

In short, select four goals that are exciting to you, achievable in the next 12 months and split into four categories—health, relationships, work/business and just for you.

If this does not get you down to four goals, become really ruthless. You want to choose the goals that matter the most, that will compel you to achieve them. Choose four and sever the rest.

Small is the Key to it All

Why did you go big just to go small? You brainstormed a massive wish list to get you actually thinking about what you want in life. You cannot start to figure out HOW to get what you want until you are able to ascertain WHAT you want. Clarity is power.

Then you went small so you could invite your subconscious and the universe to come up with ideas to make your dreams into realities. This won't happen with a ton of ideas—the extreme focus is essential.

At this stage the goals don't have to be written well or look pretty. You will sort that out in the next chapter in which you are going to write out the goals in a way that makes them so engaging you can't help but be motivated to take action.

Action Steps

Write down your goals wish list.

Select four goals from the list you want to tackle in the next 12 months.

8

WRITE YOUR FOUR SUPER SEXY GOALS

> *'In the beginner's mind there are many possibilities but in the expert's there are few.'* – Shunryu Suzuki

A Dirty Little Secret

Here is a secret I probably should have told you earlier. It doesn't really matter which four goals you choose. Yes they should be appealing, but don't worry if you don't feel as passionate about them as you think you should be. Do not stress if you don't think they are the most magnificent goals ever. Just choose four things you want. Pick four and be done with it.

Once you start taking action on these four goals and see them being accomplished, your belief that goal setting can have a positive, even profound impact on your life will be created. Four goals, no matter what they entail, no matter if they are big or small or purple or green gives you a better chance at seeing that the actions you take bring about fulfillment and success.

Next year you are much more likely to pull out that big wish list you put away and select four more goals to try and achieve. Goal setting then becomes a powerful habit in your life.

So pick four goals. Any four. Now you are going to write them out in a way that makes it impossible not to take action on them.

Challenge Yourself

Another thing before we get into the nitty gritty of actually writing out your top four goals in the sexiest way possible. Now is a good time to look at your goals and decide if they are challenging enough but not too challenging.

The tip here is to lean towards making them more challenging than less. If you have written that you want to win an Olympic medal, play a violin solo at Carnegie Hall or take a rocket ship to Mars, then you may want to scale that goal back. You only have one year!

But if your goals don't give you a jittery feeling, then aim a bit higher. If you don't achieve that exact perfect end goal, you will have likely achieved more than you would have done otherwise. You have written half of a novel? Great, you have gone further than most people.

When a goal is slightly beyond what you consider achievable, it forces you to work out ways to make it possible. More on this later, but you can ask others to help, or commit yourself fully to your goal for a set period, or find a person who has achieved what you want and mimic them. You will be surprised how much you can accomplish in just one year.

Three Types of Goals

You have likely written your goals in one of three ways:

End Goal

This is the final piece of the puzzle or rung of the ladder. It is what makes the goal feel complete, a success. For example: win a marathon, write a New York Times best seller or watch a spectacular sunset over Maui. These paint a great picture of goal completion, but the trouble is that the final step of the goal is out of your hands. You may be running against an Olympian, publish your book on the same day as a new Harry Potter or visit Maui in rainy season. You can use parts of this end goal picture in your goal writing, but don't rely on it to feel like you have successfully completed the goal. After all, winning the lottery can be a goal, but if it is out of your hands to succeed at it, it becomes rather meaningless.

Performance Goal

This is describing what you would like to achieve when you finish the goal. It is slightly different from above as it is mostly within your control. For example: complete the marathon in a certain time frame, publish the book and get in the top ten in an Amazon category, have a cocktail on the beach in Maui. It may seem slightly less exciting than an end goal above, but it makes for a compelling and attainable goal.

Process Goal

This tells you what you have to do to achieve the goal. Effectively these can be thought of as the actions you take, or the habits you build or mini-goals. For example: run 10 miles three times per week, write at least 1000 words every day, save a certain amount of money each week for the trip to Maui. When you are writing out your ultimate goal, you will exclude these, but they become important when you are writing your action plan, which is covered in the next chapter.

Super Sexy Elements

A super sexy goal has three elements: powerful language, a vivid description and an emotional connection weaved in. Let us look at these parts of the written goal in a bit more detail.

Powerful Language

Be very clear and specific about what you want. State the goal in the positive, use action words and include an exact deadline. Be concise—one or two sentences are enough.

Vivid Description

Create a brief description that conveys in an action replay type way exactly what you will be doing when your goal is reached. Super sexy tip—if you can't imagine it, then think about the Facebook status update you will write. When I decided to do the fire walk, I couldn't begin to imagine what the whole experience would be like, but I knew I could write 'I am now a firewalker' on Facebook.

EMOTION AND MEANING

Weave into the short, powerful, vivid description the meaning the goal has for you—why you will feel so happy or successful or excited when you achieve it. Add a sprinkle of emotion—your exact feelings as your goal is reached. This is all tied in with your 'why', your purpose that will be fleshed out with the action steps later. But for now, add a taste of your emotional connection to the goal.

THIS MAY SEEM LIKE A LOT TO PACK INTO A COUPLE OF sentences, but it is really simple if you use the following templates.

TEMPLATES AND EXAMPLES

Here are two super sexy templates that I use to write goals that carry all these elements. Pick what resonates with you, get your four goals and rewrite them using the templates and examples below. Remember only do this with your top four goals. You will run out of steam if you try to do this with the entire goals wish list.

> It is (future date) and I am/ I have (end step). I am feeling...
>
> I am so happy and grateful that (goal success) on or before (date). [Vivid description of goal].

Here are some examples of my own goals using the templates above:

> It is November 2008 and I have just completed the Auckland half marathon in less than 2 ½ hours. I am feeling great and my support team is patting me on the back and telling me well done.
>
> It is October 2015 and I have just sold the very first copy of my first book. I am feeling excited as I know this is just the beginning of a new way to earn income.
>
> It is the end of July 2017 and I have just stood on the scales ten pounds lighter than the start of the year. I am a lot more energized with my focus on exercise and healthy eating.
>
> I am so happy and grateful that I have bought my first investment property on or before March 2009. I am standing in the empty house, thinking this is all mine, and opening a bottle of champagne.
>
> I am so happy and grateful that I travelled around Croatia on or before September 2010. I am lying on the beach in sun-drenched Croatia and reading a fantastic book, just relaxing and enjoying the sun.
>
> I am so happy and grateful that I have published a children's picture book on or before October 2017. I have just received the first five-star review of my beautiful book and am feeling so happy that it is out in the world for kids and their parents to enjoy.

One Year, Four Goals

Here is one illustration of four super sexy goals using the templates in the suggested categories—health, relationships, work, and 'just for you'.

> Health: I am so happy and grateful that I am more fit than I have been in the past five years on or before July 2018. I have just completed a gym workout and am feeling fit, strong, toned and full of energy.
>
> Relationship: It is August 2018 and I am on the eighth date of this year with my husband. We are out at our favorite local restaurant talking and laughing and feeling more connected than ever.
>
> Work/Business: I am so happy and grateful that I have published three Amazon best-selling books on or before October 2018. I have just taken a screen shot of my new book showing it is in the top 10 in its Amazon category.
>
> Just for You: It is the end of November 2018 and I am reading my new children's picture book to my son's class at school. I am feeling happy that I have produced something beautiful and fun for kids to enjoy.

The astute among you may have realized that I have just shared my top four super sexy goals for this year with you all! Everyone who reads this book can now hold me accountable. More on accountability soon.

Note that I didn't write a goal about my kids or my home or my friends. This does not imply that they are any less important in my day-to-day life. It is simply that there is not a goal around them for this year.

Another Dirty Little Secret

Just because you write your goals in this way doesn't guarantee success. But it sure gives them more of a prospect. When a goal, any goal, achieves fruition, it is rather miraculous. If you attempt all four this year and only get one, isn't it still worth a try?

Writing down a goal that doesn't end up as the success you wanted is hard. Not writing down any goals and living an average life (broke and unhappy) is hard. <u>Choose your hard</u>.

> In summary: write out a brief, informative, emotionally-charged goal you would be happy to say out loud.

Do this because you want your goals to be so irresistible that you cannot NOT tackle them. It is a no brainer to embark on them. Do this because you are creating a big enough reason to figure out the how. This how, this taking action, is covered in the next chapter.

Action Step

Write down your four super sexy goals for the next 12 months using the templates.

9
TAKE ACTION (EAT ELEPHANTS AND FROGS)

> 'The most effective way to do it, is to do it.' – Amelia Earhart

Nom Nom Nom

There seems to be an obsession with devouring animals in goal-setting literature. Breaking goals into small steps is depicted as eating an elephant 'one bite at a time'. We are told to 'eat that frog' when we tackle the hardest or most impactful task first.

Maybe taking action is described in metaphors because it is more romantic than thinking of all the hard work that is involved. Yes, taking action may be the least sexy part of super sexy goals, as you have to actually DO something.

This chapter explains how this part can be, if not fun, at least easy and painless.

• • •

RPM

You have written a super sexy goal—a RESULT you want to see. You now want to add in the PURPOSE behind it and a MASSIVE ACTION PLAN. This RPM—Results, Purpose, Massive Action Plan method is recommended by author, coach and personal development expert, Tony Robbins. After 40 years of coaching everyone from people on the verge of suicide to presidents, he knows a thing or two about achieving goals, so why not try it?

Writing out the purpose or 'why' behind your goals gives you extra motivation to achieve them. Do not skip this step! It is where your emotional juice is. When the going gets tough, reading your why may be the only thing that gets you through. Move beyond the literal answer and get to how you want to feel.

The massive action plan is a big picture overview of the main actions to achieve your goal. It is the 'map'. These actions don't have to be in order, be prioritized or be scheduled. You will do this next. For now, it is about getting them down.

This is best illustrated in an example. Here are two of my previous goals written using the RPM method:

HEALTH

Goal (Result):

It is the end of July 2017 and I have just stood on the scales ten pounds lighter than the start of the year. I am a lot more energized with my focus on exercise and healthy eating.

Why? (Purpose):

- I have the strength and energy to do all the things I want to do
- What I put in my body is very important to my energy and wellbeing

How? (Massive Action Plan):

- Green drink – every weekday
- Go to the gym or for a walk every day
- Create a vegetarian dinner at least once per week
- No alcohol during the week
- No sugar after dinner
- Try a vegetable juice fast for at least one day
- Do the Color Run
- Do the Wanderlust 'triathlon'

WRITING - CHILDREN

Goal (Result):

I am so happy and grateful that I have published a children's picture book on or before October 2017. I have just received the first five-star review of my beautiful book.

Why? (Purpose):

- Fun to write something that kids will love
- Want to show that it is possible to self-publish a great picture book

How? (Massive Action Plan):

- Collate and format *Maxy Moo* book

- Get a book launch team together
- Launch the book out into the world
- Read book to local daycare

Notice that the number of bullet points varies. I could easily think of a lot of specific ways to get healthier, but as I had never produced a picture book before, the action steps involved were fewer and more vague.

Brainstorm a few reasons why you are embarking on each of the four goals and decide on a few of the main actions that you will take. Do not take ages on this; give yourself an hour or so at the most. You can change your reasons and action steps if they are not working for you. Just get something down so you can start prioritizing and scheduling.

Prioritizing

You now have a handful of action items, but what is the best one to do first? The trouble with a lot of goal setting books is that they tell you to write the goal and then formulate the whole action plan to achieve them. As if you would suddenly and immaculately know all the action steps in the right order to get the goal you want!

Actually it is better if you don't know. If I had known everything I would have to do to make that half marathon run happen, I don't think I would have attempted it. It is important to be able to work out some chunks of action when you write your goals, but for now you need to take the first step.

Most people have heard of Pareto's principle—the 80/20 rule—that 80% of results often come from 20% of actions or tasks. Think about what that 20% is for your goals. In fact, go even more focused than that. In Gary Keller and Jay Papasan's book *The One Thing*, it is stated that we should ask this powerful question:

> 'What is the ONE thing (right now) I can do such that by doing it everything else would be easier or unnecessary?'

It is extreme Pareto—the 20% of the 20% of the 20% to the single most important ONE thing. This identifies what they call the 'lead domino'. The domino at the start of the chain that creates a domino effect when it is pushed over. Figure out the 'lead domino' and then whack away at it until it falls and other dominos fall in sequence, too. Look, you may not know what this is, but take an educated guess. Listen to your intuition.

For my health goal last year this was eliminating sugar completely out of my diet. You will notice the action step in my original plan said no sugar after dinner, but at the start of May last year, I took processed sugar out of my diet completely. This led to more energy, to wanting to go for a walk or to the gym each day and to finding more healthy food alternatives, especially at snack time. For the children's picture book goal this was deciding to pay a designer to collate and format the book rather than doing it myself. That freed up my time for things I could do well, like gathering a launch team, and meant the book was ready in a shorter time and looked more beautiful than anything I could have produced on my own.

> What is your ONE thing or lead domino action step for each of your four goals?

Scheduling

We are now at the pinnacle of the least sexy part of goal setting. Putting the most important action steps in your calendar. Don't run away now! You have come so far. First, it doesn't matter what sort of calendar or diary system you use—digital or traditional, daily, weekly, monthly, or yearly. Just get it in there.

Take a big picture view of the next 12 months with all your scheduled appointments and plans in your diary or calendar. Decide on when you will devote time to your goals and block out those times as well. You may want to block out 15 minutes each weekday or a half-day each weekend, for example.

Once you figure out your first tasks or 'lead dominos', add a short description into your blocked out times. This may be best just for the first month or two. Do not worry if you are not sure what the task is or how long it will take to finish it. Just shade out time. Treat it like another appointment and make yourself unavailable.

Then try to stick to your schedule. Yes, you may not get that task done in the time you have available, but you have started to 'eat the elephant'. And yes, life can take over—your child gets sick or you have an emergency dental appointment—but if you don't schedule it, it definitely won't happen. At least if it is in the diary or calendar, there is a likelihood of spending time on it.

Review on a daily, weekly or monthly basis. I find reviewing and rescheduling on a weekly basis best for me so I will detail this method. On Sunday evening I spend about 20 minutes looking at the week ahead. I put in my work, exercise, scheduled appointments, kids' activities and anything else that I know will happen. Then I work out one or two most important tasks from my Massive Action Plan and time block them. This can be 10 minutes to full days.

Top Tips to Take Action

Here are six tips to help make choosing, prioritizing and scheduling actions even easier:

Give Up Something

Perhaps you are trying to be the 'busy champion of the world' and there is NO WAY you can squeeze in even taking one bite of the elephant into your already full to overflowing life. Give something up that keeps you playing small. It doesn't have to be forever, but give it up for a week and see if that helps. Stop watching the news every night; cancel that subscription to a magazine you never read, or change the notification settings on your social media accounts. You can do something about removing the superfluous busy things that do not add any value to your life. I have recently taken the Facebook app off my phone and it has stopped me from compulsively checking it many times a day. Essentially, you are sacrificing some instant gratification for an end goal that creates much more value ('sexiness') in your life. Believe me, it is worth it.

Use Your Calendar

Utilize your calendar or diary system in the best way possible. If there is ONE thing you want to get done today that moves you toward your goals, some people find that writing that on a Post-It note and placing it where they see it is helpful. Then you can rip the Post-It note off the computer or wall and scrunch it up in a burst of enthusiasm when that task is checked off. If you want to do something every day towards your goals (go for a walk, write 1,000 words, etc.), then get a wall calendar and 'don't break the chain'. Put a cross on the calendar for every day you take action and try to keep that chain of crosses going. I can't tell you how helpful 'don't break the chain' is for writing the first draft of a book.

TRY AN 'IF-THEN' PLAN

If you are not sure exactly when you can assign time to a goal task for the week, then try an 'if-then' plan. This is spelled out in the excellent book, *Succeed* by Heidi Grant Halvorson. Tell yourself if your partner is taking your child to her sports game, then you will go for a run. But if you are taking her, then you can spend half the time of the game on writing your book. If you finish work late, you will commit to a ten-minute walk, but if you get out on time, you will go to that hour-long class at the gym.

JUST DO ONE

Do one tiny little thing to start you off. Can't face 20 push-ups? Commit to doing just one. You have time for one push up. An old idea is to floss just one tooth. Give yourself permission to finish after one. You have taken the action you said you would take for the day. Usually you will continue, but you are a success in what you set out to do regardless.

· · ·

Don't Eat that Frog

We are told to 'eat that frog'—do the hardest or most impactful task first. But sometimes eating that frog seems too daunting. So don't. Do a secondary task that doesn't exert as much willpower but still brings you closer to the goal. Invite people to join your book launch team instead of writing the next chapter. Walk instead of jog. Have date night in the living room instead of trying to dress up and find babysitters. Don't do this all the time, but if you are tired, then don't feel the need to over exert yourself. The last thing you want is to stop the momentum entirely. At least this way you can feel like you are doing something that moves you forward.

Kill Two Birds with One Stone

The absolute best tip is to work out some high-impact activities. Can you schedule something in that goes towards two or more goals at the same time? For instance, you could have a brisk game of tag outside with your children, thus checking off health (exercise) and relationships (quality time with kids).

Schedule Your Dreams

Dream big and then schedule your dreams. Sure, organization and time management don't seem sexy.

> Consistently choosing in favor of what you really want and feeling energized with a new purpose—now that IS sexy.

Just start. This creates a ripple effect. And when you are in motion you can see the next action step, the next domino. You are not as far away from your goals as you may think you are. It is not a big leap, but small changes—each tiny bite of the elephant—that bring even the most far-fetched goal into reach.

By now you may have encountered some issues with goals. This is good news as it means goal setting is working! The next chapter tackles three of the main problems you may face.

Action Steps

Write down your RPM plan for each of your four super sexy goals.

Work out the first thing to focus on ('the lead domino') for each of the goals.

Shade out some time in your diary or calendar to work on your goals.

Review your diary or calendar and your scheduled tasks on a consistent basis.

10

GOAL SETTING PROBLEMS AND SOLUTIONS

> 'We are all in the gutter, but some of us are looking at the stars.' – Oscar Wilde

The Bad News

I have some bad news for you. Even with the most appealing and meaningful goals, the most focused commitment and the best prioritizing and scheduling structure for taking action, you WILL encounter problems.

This system does everything in its power to set up the goals for the best chance at success, but it is important to realize that at times this won't be easy and you will have to learn to deal with issues along the way. Having goals does not eliminate problems, but hopefully it gives you better quality problems!

Here are three main goal-setting problems and some tips and tools to overcome them.

· · ·

Obstacles

You are at the start of your goal. Day one. The first step. And way in the distance, around all those bends and over those hills and down through those valleys is your goal. With those many miles between you and your goal, it is obvious that there will be obstacles on the way to achieving it.

Most people don't set goals. I understand that. But then, unfortunately, of the small number of people who embark on goals, many give them up at the first major hurdle.

Obstacles can come in many different forms and be in all areas—from limitations in money, resources and time, to loved ones being negative about the goal. What happens when people encounter obstacles? Often they stop or go back, or even more ridiculously, but very commonly, they carry the obstacle around with them as some sort of 'proof' that they shouldn't be going for the goal!

You have a car breakdown that wipes out all your travel savings. Or you have a fight with your spouse on your first date night in two years, or a dog chases you on your morning run. So you tell yourself that it was not meant to be or it is too ambitious or ask, 'Who am I to want something like that?'

No matter what type of obstacle you encounter, the first thing that needs to change is your beliefs about obstacles. Your mindset in this area needs a complete overhaul if you are ever going to succeed in your goals.

> Obstacles are actually fan-flippin-tastic!

You WANT to have obstacles! Obstacles don't exist until you set goals, and they only start to show up when you are on the way to achieving your goals. So you should get really excited, as they show you that goal setting works—it is taking you somewhere.

Here are some tips on overcoming obstacles. When you first set a goal, studies have proven that the best mindset is to be positive about success but not about how easy it will be. You need to be positive that it will be tough and there will be obstacles. You don't have to know (and won't know) every obstacle in advance, but you can prepare for some of them. When I ran the half-marathon I knew my feet needed extra care and I spent money on appropriate footwear and podiatrist visits. Just know that in your head you will have a kind of mental contrast in which you hold onto the positivity of how it will be when you achieve the goal and also maintain realistic thoughts about what it will really take to get there.

Flexibility is the key to goal setting. You don't expect to move in a straight line anywhere else in life, so why would goal setting be any different? Adjustments and course corrections will be required. If your environment doesn't support your goals, what can you do to change your environment? Can you sell your unreliable car and take public transport, go to the movies with your spouse instead of talking over dinner or run along a different route?

One major obstacle many people encounter is negative reactions from others. Remember what was said earlier in the objections chapter. You OWE it to the world to use the gifts and resources you have been bestowed. Otherwise you have been given the golden ticket and thrown it away.

You may be worried about how all this change is going to affect your loved ones. Honestly, if you don't tell them about your goals, at least not straight away, your partner, kids, family and friends may not notice at all. If there is a comment or even friction, explain that you are working on becoming a better person. Tell them you are going to be the same person but more YOU: less distracted, less stressed, happier and more fun. How could anyone say they wouldn't like that? If there is still some conflict, realize that their reactions are just coming from their own needs, and you have the power to respond in the most resourceful way you can.

You may still be wondering how to tackle a specific obstacle that has arisen. Overcoming obstacles is a muscle that you need to build up. The more you do it, the easier it will be. As long as you frame obstacles as a good thing, you are halfway there already.

When to Give Up?

How to choose whether to give up or keep going with a goal can be a big issue in goal setting. But the answer to this is simple. IF and only if the goal is costing you too much—in that it doesn't reflect the real you, is causing significant sacrifice in most other areas of your life, is taking up all your time with no end in sight, or is making you deeply unhappy or unwell—can you give it up. That is it.

Too big a sacrifice means give up. If you don't want to do a particularly unpleasant but necessary action step of a goal, or if you encounter any other obstacle, no matter how enormous, keep going.

My friend Barry took on an incredible goal at the start of last year—he planned to hike up to Mount Everest basecamp in Nepal, over 5,300m or 17,500 feet above sea level. Unfortunately, seven days into the trek, Barry developed a lung infection caused by the freezing temperatures. That combined with mild food poisoning meant that he had to make the difficult decision not to continue. He was at Gorak-Shep, over 5,000m or almost 17,000 feet above sea level, less than a three-hour hike from Everest basecamp.

You would perhaps think that he would be devastated by not achieving his ultimate goal, but he is actually on cloud nine about the whole experience. He does not regret a single thing. He is amazed with his mental fortitude—he says he climbed with his mind, not his legs. He became better at decision making and overcoming unexpected challenges. He is pleased with what his body could handle—even in dusty or freezing conditions. He got closer to his hiking club friends who came on the trip, and at 51 is fitter than he has ever been. Plus he felt a profound sense of being alive in the magnificent mountain landscape.

> Set some goals because even if you give up on them, they will likely have a lasting impact on your life.

One thing you should contemplate up front is how much of a 'follow through' kind of person you are. Some people do about 80% of something and then delegate the rest or decide it is good enough to be thought of as finished. Others have to dot every I and cross every T to feel done. Knowing how well you follow through will help you decide if this giving up idea is just a pattern that repeats a lot in your life—one that may not serve you all that well.

When you are on the road to improving a skill or mastering something, everyone gets a burst of progress and then a plateau. You will get stronger in your new fitness regime but then not change weights for a while. You will get a couple of quick promotions and then not move upwards for ages. The most successful people know that the plateau is just a stage in the goal and not a reason to give up. They will look at alternative ways to move past the plateau to another growth period, even if it means going sideways or backwards for a bit. Learn to respect the plateau stage, as it is part of the mastery.

Sometimes people put a lot of hard work into a goal only to realize they are too far down the wrong path and have to give up. The key to making sure this doesn't happen is to regularly review your goals. Check in with whether you are in the right place and course correct as necessary. This is failing on a small scale; failing forward, and hopefully will avoid a big 'Should I give up?' later on. You may feel that if you stop to check how you are doing, you will lose momentum or get some feedback you don't want, but this is a lesser issue than proceeding in the wrong direction until you reach a destination you did not want to visit.

If you give up on a goal, focus on the other three goals, and if it works, add a new goal into the mix. Please don't give up on all your goals if one doesn't work out.

COMPETING GOALS

One major way you can trip yourself up is to have competing goals. You help this by first being aware that it can be an issue. Many people don't even think about it. You can also try to decide on goals that complement each other when you brainstorm and write them. And as noted in the previous chapter, you can stack actions to check off more than one goal at a time. But at times goals will compete for your attention and resources; it is baked into your busy life, so what do you do about this problem?

First, understand that a balanced life is a myth. Extraordinary results require focused attention and time, and that means time away from other things, so that makes balance impossible.

If you have a looming deadline, know that sometimes one goal will take priority for a while. Whatever you do, do NOT neglect your health for too long—healthy food, exercise and enough sleep are critical—or ALL your goals will fall down.

Most importantly, if your self-control reserves are low, don't pursue two goals at once that both require a lot of self-control. If you want to write a novel and run a marathon in the same year and you have done neither before, then consider concentrating on one in the first half of the year and the other in the second half, for example, rather than both of them for the entire 12 months.

Having no more than four goals will help to reduce the chance of competing goals and goal overwhelm in general. If it helps, only focus on one, two or three goals, at least for a time. Knowing that goal conflicts are a common issue and they are not an excuse to give up or fail at your goals should also help considerably.

Having conflicting goals is hard at times. Having no goals at all because of a goal conflict and staying in your average life is hard. <u>Choose your hard.</u>

THE GOOD NEWS

When you step out of your comfort zone and strive to reach your potential you will encounter mess. Being okay with chaos is an essential element of successfully completing goals.

> Breathe through the chaos.

Remember your Lizard mind is not used to all this positive action and progressing forward. It likes you to stay tucked up in your little comfort zone. It bombards you with negative thinking that any problem automatically means goal failure and necessitates retreat.

You now have everything you need to successfully counter Lizard thinking. Well-written, vividly-painted and emotionally-charged goals. Reasons why your goals will bring you fulfillment and success. Action steps with ways to prioritize and schedule tasks. Plus ways to handle the main goal-setting problems that arise.

> You have no excuses—start on your goals today!

A few strategies to guarantee goal success are covered in the next chapter. This is the penultimate chapter before we wrap everything up in one last sexy chapter.

11

SUPERCHARGE YOUR SUPER SEXY GOALS

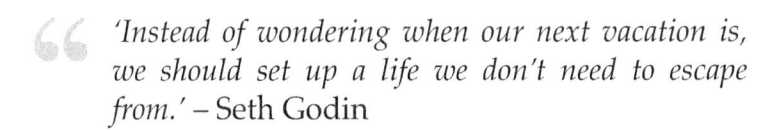

> *'Instead of wondering when our next vacation is, we should set up a life we don't need to escape from.'* – Seth Godin

Meta Goal

I can't tell you how much deadlines, rewards and accountability helped in finishing writing the first draft of this book. I told everyone my plan to finish the first draft before Christmas and then take a few days off over the festive season as a reward of sorts. After all, it almost seems compulsory to have a goal when you are writing a book on goal setting!

Sure, the Christmas deadline was of my own making. Sure, I could have still worked on it over the festive break. And sure, not many people would hold me accountable as most people are rushing around at Christmas time and are unlikely to remember what I said in passing about writing a book.

But these three strategies directed my attention to the most important thing for me—getting the first draft of this book written. I gave up things, I delegated, and I stayed up a little later than I normally would. But I achieved my goal. And it felt pretty darn good.

You will encounter problems when going for your goals, but you also have a lot of power to do everything you can to make them happen. Here are nine top tools that will help you achieve your super sexy goals.

Deadlines

Everyone has experienced the power of a deadline at some stage in his or her life. From a due date on an essay to a work project, having a deadline makes it easier to aim at something. As noted above they can be artificial—a date you have plucked out that seems like a reasonable time by which to get your goal done. Or they can be imposed from the outside—a triathlon race date for example.

The most important thing to remember with deadlines is to not beat yourself up too much if you don't hit them. Don't give yourself a pass to let them fly by every single time, but if you have to move the goal posts, it is not usually the end of the world.

Especially if it is something you haven't done before, you may only have a vague notion of the effort it can take. I thought it would take two months to publish my children's picture book, *Maxy-Moo Flies to the Moon*. Instead it took me close to two years to get it out into the world. It was still worth it in the end, and in fact, the long anticipation of seeing that goal come to fruition made the book launch even better.

Sometimes, when you achieve a goal before the looming deadline hits, you feel like a rock star. This is particularly true if it seems impossible. National Novel Writing Month (NaNoWriMo) challenges people to write a 50,000-word (approximately 200-page) novel in a month. When I signed up for the challenge I thought there was no chance I would accomplish such a feat in such a short amount of time. I got to 50,000 words with a couple of days to spare. Sure, my silly romance is unlikely to be published in its current state, but I wrote a novel and not everyone can say that.

The super sexy goal setting system gives you 12 months to complete your goals. This is arbitrary, but it is a finite period in which you can achieve something worthy. Sometimes it is better to make the deadline shorter rather than longer as you don't strive for perfection or procrastinate and just actually finish something. Overall, though, if you get somewhere, anywhere on the journey to your ultimate goal before your deadline, it is better than not doing anything.

Rewards

Rewards and incentives, when used in the right way, can be a very powerful method to aid in enjoying each step to accomplishing a goal.

In theory at least, internal drivers are much more important than external rewards. There are three keys for keeping motivation high: knowing the purpose behind the task, mastery of the task and autonomy (control over the task). Remember pull motivation? You want to have some of this baked into the goals you have set so they are intrinsically rewarding.

Sometimes you just need a bit more help, so what else can you do? Use push motivation methods. Have a built-in celebration system. Celebrate in small ways any task completed or mini goal achieved. Pat yourself on the back, indulge in some rest time or take a walk in the sunshine.

For bigger milestones amp up the rewards. This is especially important when you have had to do something very challenging or difficult and the intrinsic rewards have dried up. Go out for dinner, buy yourself some flowers or indulge in that latest binge-watching sensation. Do something nice for yourself. It is best if you don't rely on this method; only do it occasionally so you can feel like it is an unexpected benefit.

Of course, we should all be falling in love with the journey as well as the dream goal. So constantly ask yourself how you can make the action more fun or enjoyable. Remember, this is what successful people do. Run on the treadmill while listening to your favorite podcast. Or keep a gratitude journal about your goals and life. Savor how much getting to the end of something means to you by taking a photo of the occasion or bragging to someone about it. If you keep up a positive attitude, the whole thing is a win no matter what.

Accountability

Telling people about your goals can have its downsides if done incorrectly, but done right it can improve your chances of success by up to 80%, or twice as much as just writing them down, depending on which study you read.

Two things you must be aware of before you share your goals. First, choose people who are more likely to support your goals. Being an accountability partner for someone requires time and effort, so choose him or her wisely. You want someone who gives you attention, motivation, information, inspiration, feedback and expertise. Look to friends who have achieved similar goals or be prepared to pay for a mentor or a coach.

In addition, share your goal in a way that makes your brain think you still have to actually do the goal. As entrepreneur and author, Derek Sivers, notes in his short TEDx talk 'Keep your goals to yourself', you need to have a future tense way of stating the goal, otherwise your mind thinks the goal is done and releases the tension required to take action. Don't tell people that you are running a marathon race soon. Rephrase it: 'I really need to train for this upcoming marathon'.

Decide on the best way to update your accountability partners—a daily text, a weekly Skype session or a monthly email update—and then commit to that. Tell them what you want from them, what questions they should ask and what they should follow up on. Be prepared to hear not just support and encouragement but hard truths and constructive criticism. They are not friends in this capacity; they are your accountability partners.

If you don't want to tell people what you are doing, you can find other ways to hold yourself accountable. Use a journal to log your progress. Or keep an anonymous profile on a site like stickk.com, which gives you options of rewards for achieving or punishments for not achieving your goals. You can program into stickk.com that you will donate money to a charity you don't like or give money to some of your friends if you don't get to your goal by your deadline. The 'carrot' method of using rewards combined with a literal stick method at stickk.com can work extremely well.

Review Your Goals Regularly

Deadlines, rewards and accountability are the three main tools I used to write this very book, but there are plenty of other tools that you can use to supercharge your goal success.

Make sure you have your super sexy goals list somewhere you have easy access to it and see it every day. Use a pen and paper version or print it out and stick it to your wall, on the fridge or on the bathroom mirror. For those who are more private, stick it inside the door to your wardrobe or tuck it into a journal you write in regularly. One pro tip is to sign your name at the bottom of the list. This seems silly, but it makes it a contract with yourself and somehow this makes it seem more legitimate.

If you have an electronic Word document or PDF of your list, then place that document on your computer desktop, or add it into your notes or books apps on your phone so you can open it up and read it regularly.

Some of you may want to share your goals list on your favorite social media feed, on Pinterest or on your own blog. Sharing it and getting others involved keeps you even more accountable, but as noted above, it does have a potential downside in that some people may be less than enthusiastic about your new pursuits.

A fun and completely optional way to display your goals list is to create a 'vision board' of it. A vision board is any sort of board on which you display images that represent your goals list items—what you want to do, see and master. Create one the old-fashioned way out of cut outs from magazines stuck to a big piece of paper or cardboard. Or combine some pictures into an online board on Pinterest or elsewhere.

An extra cool idea is to take a photo of your written goals list or its physical vision board and upload it so it becomes your computer screen saver or wallpaper on your phone. We look at our phones on average over 100 times a day, so the goals list will be reviewed, at least subconsciously, an enormous amount.

Alternatively, be more active in reviewing your goals. Ask yourself powerful questions such as 'what is one thing I can do today to help me achieve this goal?' Recite the goals as affirmations in a confident voice. Read the goal then close your eyes and visualize what the scene will be like when it is achieved. Bask in that visualization for a few moments.

Choose to read, review and display your goals list in a way that reflects you. The point is to not forget your goals. They will become more real the more you review them and then you are more likely to take action.

Role Models

Goals are particularly difficult when you are embarking on something you have never done before. One way to help with this is to find someone who is doing or has already achieved what you want and use them as a role model. This can be a real-life friend, someone in a book you read, a famous person whom you look up to or a coach. You want to find someone who is successful at what you want to do. You will be amazed at how much information you can find out about their strategies just from reading books or articles or searching online.

Channeling role models helps you shift your identity. It makes you think about the person you want to BE rather than just what you want to DO. Take some of your role model's determination or strength or grace as well as their strategies and utilize it for your own benefit.

> We don't get our goals, we get who we think
> we are.

One caveat here is to work at your own pace and reach the goal you want. If someone you are modeling is out of this world successful, you may never reach that level. But if you move to attain even one percent of their success, then you are ahead of where you were, and that is the only thing that is important. Play your own game, no one else's.

Say NO

It has already been mentioned that you will have to give up stuff to make way for your goals. This can be as easy as turning off the news or Twitter for a while, but sometimes when you say 'no' you have to say it directly. Saying 'no' politely but assertively is a powerful time management skill. Here are a few ways to say 'no' nicely:

> 'Sounds wonderful, but that is not part of my work focus right now.'
> 'Sorry but my current commitments mean I cannot take that on.'
> 'It sounds amazing but I wouldn't be able to give that the attention it deserves.'

'I can't help you right now but can schedule it after X date.'

Another way to say 'no' is to call it a policy: 'Sorry it is not my policy to do (such and such)'. People respect policies, even ones you have made up yourself, and you just said 'no' without even actually saying no!

Even in the nicest way possible, saying 'no' is uncomfortable so practice on small things and build up.

> If you do not learn to say 'no', then you are saying YES to someone else's agenda and NO to yourself.

You will know in your gut if 'no' is the right answer. If you are unsure, give it the 'Hell Yeah!' test. As Derek Sivers (quoted twice in the same chapter, lucky him) says, 'if it's not a hell yeah, it is a NO'.

If a 'no' is done well, people should be happy with how clear you are and how committed you are to what is important to you. And, well, if they are not, too bad. Their response is their problem.

Routines

Having goals sets you up for a large amount of decision making and mental strain. You may not be able to get out of the extra stamina required to attain goals, but you can take out any extra energy from other parts of your life so you don't feel overwhelmed.

Having the same routine is one way to spend less energy on things that are not as important as your goals and if done right also makes sure you look after your personal wellbeing. A good routine is to go to bed at the same time each night. Some successful people take this further and have the same thing for breakfast each morning or wear similar outfits every day.

Another way to build routine into goal setting is to have triggers or anchors that create an environment that the goal task is underway. I have a classical music playlist and when I put those headphones on, I know it is book-writing time.

Go Hard at First

Personal development expert, Tony Robbins, states that the path to mastery starts with a period of total immersion then continues with scheduled repetition. He asserts that if you commit to doing something just five times in a row, such as going to the gym every day, this will create momentum and you will continue with it. So if you want to learn something new, then go to the dance or painting or judo class every night for a week or commit to at least ten lessons in one month. After that scale it back.

This period of intensity is temporary, just enough to convert your willpower into a positive habit. Success can be thought of as a sprint fueled by discipline just long enough for habit to kick in and take over. When you see disciplined people, you are really seeing people who have trained a handful of powerful habits into their lives, usually by this immersion technique.

During this intense stage of learning really lean into your support network. Delegate or eliminate what is not important for this limited time in your life. Ask your spouse to cook or pay for a meal delivery service. Get your kids to do chores or pay for a cleaner. Do whatever it takes to get past that first uncertain stage of skill building and then work at a less reckless pace from there.

This may seem contradictory to the 'just do one small thing' advice earlier, but it is not. Taking small actions is for when you need to keep going but may be worn out by day-to-day tasks. Going hard is for when you are in the initial stages of your goal and you are still incredibly motivated and excited.

Have Fun

Fun is not just a 'nice to have' but also an essential part of goal setting. Studies have shown that incorporating fun into goals not only increases satisfaction but actual performance of the goal by a considerable amount.

Don't worry that scheduling fun stops it being fun. Fun is fun and we all need more of it. If that means being less spontaneous by blocking out time for it, then that is what is required.

Fortunately, fun is woven into the fabric of the super sexy goal system, as there is a goal just for you that should be at least a little fun, even if it is a challenge as well. In addition, an emphasis on enjoyment is now part of your new mindset around goals. After all, successful people constantly ask 'how can I enjoy this?' and resolve to remain positive about tasks that the average person doesn't like and want to do.

Include fun in your life outside of your goals, have it as a part of the 'just for you' goal, enjoy checking off your goals and strive to be positive on the journey towards them. Simply, have fun.

• • •

Cherry on the Top

These are really powerful tools that are the cherry on the top of an already robust and sexy goal-setting system. Just know they are there and can be retrieved from the toolbox when required.

12

THE REAL GOAL OF THIS BOOK

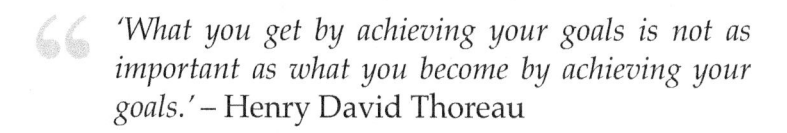

> *'What you get by achieving your goals is not as important as what you become by achieving your goals.'* – Henry David Thoreau

THIS BOOK IS A SUCCESS IF...

Getting a goal is about stepping out of your comfort zone, facing your fears and going for it. If you take action, any action at all, despite your fear, then this book is a success.

Goal setting is a system for you to stop the busy overwhelm that leads to nowhere. It is a way to be clear in your life and to bat away distractions easily. It is a tool to allow you to pinpoint what you want so you can say no to things that add no value to your life. Even if you never attain any of your goals, but you pick up these skills, then this book is a success.

Taking action on goals means not conforming to society's expectations. It means quietly leaning into the whispers of what your soul truly desires and doing what is important to you. If you start rebelliously doing what you actually want to do, then this book is a success.

Writing goals is about gaining some insight, connecting with your true self and rediscovering what you desire from your life. You figure out what your strengths are and how you can use them to build a great life for you and your loved ones. It is not about changing but becoming more yourself. If you find that you are now more in touch with your authentic self, then this book is a success.

If this book has made you question your beliefs and changed your mindset around what you are capable of, then this book is, without a doubt, a success.

Happiness

Throughout this book I promised that goals will make you feel successful or accomplished or fulfilled, but I didn't promise that it would directly lead to happiness. Happiness can be attained in the most fleeting of pleasures such as the sun on your face or a child's smile.

Succeeding at something hard often gives a greater satisfaction. Working out who you are at your best improves your confidence and self-esteem. Getting stronger—in your health, mental ability and improved potential makes you proud, and being proud is a huge source of happiness.

Life is not designed to be easy, but to present you with a series of challenges to help you grow. It is growth rather than the goal that is the ultimate prize. As motivational speaker, Jim Rohn advises, 'You want to set a goal that is big enough that in the process of achieving it, you become someone worth becoming'.

Happiness is a byproduct of figuring out a meaningful life. It is a result of doing positive things that improve your life. Don't aim for happiness, aim to grow. Aim for mastery. Aim for a life well lived, not pleasantly existed.

> Live a life in which you work hard to be fulfilled and successful, and you will experience a deeper level of happiness than you ever thought possible.

Goal Setting Revolution

Motivating people to set and get goals has been the entire point of this book because I want to fire up the world and create a goal-setting revolution! I want to dramatically increase the number of people who write goals and actively strive to achieve them.

I know goal setting is not a panacea for all the world's woes. But I am certain that if more people embraced goals, we would have more outstanding and less average people in the world. More fit, wealthy and happy people ready to share their skills and creativity to bring more love and abundance to their communities.

But deep down that is not the aim of this book.

The real goal of this book is to get you to do something.

Do

Dream big and make every piece of your life the masterpiece it is meant to be because no matter how great your life is, there is another level—one of passion, gratitude, connection, joy and success.

Go beyond expectations and what you think you are capable of and the world opens up. You will discover there is so much more you can do with your mind, body, skills and talents. You may even compel others to dream big and focus on their goals, too.

And if dreaming big still seems too much, then know that modest goals on which you take action are better than aspirational dreams you do nothing about.

By now you have worked out that it doesn't matter really what goals you choose to pursue. At the very least you have some insight about yourself, have a bit of fun, learn skills you will have with you forever and possibly inspire others to live better.

Isn't that what life is all about?

So please, please, please do something. Do something different. Do something outside your comfort zone. Do something despite the fear.

Just DO.

Take action on one of your super sexy goals today.

READER GIFT: THE HAPPY20

There is no doubt that having goals will transform your life, but it is also important to remember to squeeze the best out every single day. To remind you of this, I created

THE HAPPY20
20 Free Ways to Boost Happiness in 20 Seconds or Less

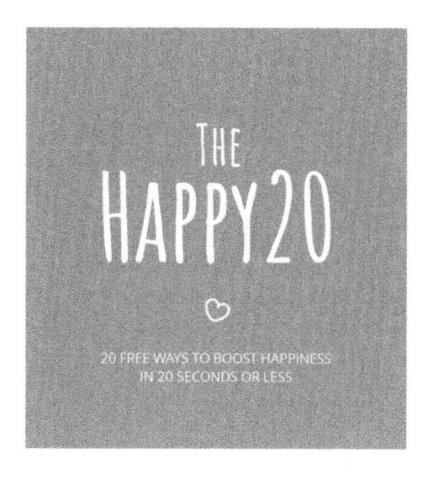

A PDF gift for you with quick ideas to improve mood and add a little sparkle to your day.

Head to **JulieSchooler.com/gift** and grab your copy today.

ABOUT THE AUTHOR

Julie had aspirations of being a writer since she was very young but somehow got sidetracked into the corporate world. After the birth of her first child, she rediscovered her creative side. You can find her at JulieSchooler.com.

Her *Easy Peasy* books provide simple and straightforward information on parenting topics. The *Nourish Your Soul* series shares delicious wisdom to feel calmer, happier and more fulfilled.

Busy people can avoid wasting time searching for often confusing and conflicting advice and instead spend time with the beautiful tiny humans in their lives and do what makes their hearts sing.

Julie lives with her family in a small, magnificent country at the bottom of the world where you may find her trying to bake the perfect chocolate brownie.

facebook.com/JulieSchoolerAuthor
instagram.com/julie.schooler
twitter.com/JulieSchooler

BOOKS BY JULIE SCHOOLER

Easy Peasy Books
Easy Peasy Potty Training
Easy Peasy Healthy Eating

Nourish Your Soul Books
Rediscover Your Sparkle
Crappy to Happy
Embrace Your Awesomeness
Bucket List Blueprint
Super Sexy Goal Setting
Find Your Purpose in 15 Minutes
Clutter-Free Forever

Children's Picture Books
Maxy-Moo Flies to the Moon

Collections
Change Your Life 3-in-1 Collection
Rebelliously Happy 3-in-1 Collection

JulieSchooler.com/books

ACKNOWLEDGMENTS

This book is the result of some serious 'kick up the proverbial' coaching by two amazing women: Joanna Penn and Louise Thompson. What Joanna doesn't know about indie publishing is not worth knowing. Louise and the Wellbeing Warriors tribe inspire me to improve every day. Thank you and Namaste.

Thanks to the many personal development seminars and workshops I have attended and all the interesting people I have high-fived at them. Knowing that there are many others in the world taking action on their goals makes me think my goal setting revolution idea has potential.

To Andrew and our two beautiful tiny humans, Dylan and Eloise. I live in a perpetual state of astonishment about how fortunate my life is. Thank you for making me laugh every single day.

PLEASE LEAVE A REVIEW

Super Sexy Goal Setting

The Fun and Simple Goals Strategy to Create a Life You Love

THANK YOU FOR READING THIS BOOK

I devoted many months to researching and writing this book. I then spent more time having it professionally edited, working with a designer to create an awesome cover and launching it into the world.

Time, money and heart has gone into this book and I very much hope you enjoyed reading it as much as I loved creating it.

It would mean the world to me if you could spend a few minutes writing a review on Goodreads or the online store where you purchased this book.

Please Leave a Review

A review can be as short or long as you like and should be helpful and honest to assist other potential buyers of the book.

Reviews provide social proof that people like and recommend the book. More book reviews mean more book sales which means I can write more books.

Your book review helps me, as an independent author, more than you could ever know. I read every single review and when I get five-star review it absolutely makes my day.

Thanks, Julie.

REFERENCES

People and Resources

Various TED and TEDx talks, podcasts and blogs on goals and goal setting

Tony Robbins

Martha Beck

Tim Ferriss

Marie Forleo

Chris Howard

Kurek Ashley

Jim Rohn

Zig Ziglar

Brian Tracey

…and many others

References

Books

59 Seconds – Change Your Life in Under a Minute – Richard Wiseman (USA, 2011)

Authentic Happiness – Using the New Positive Psychology to Realize Your Potential for Lasting Fulfillment – Martin Seligman, Ph.D. (US, 2002)

Feel the Fear and Do It Anyway – How to Turn Your Fear and Indecision into Confidence and Action – Susan Jeffers (UK, 1987)

Minimalism – Live a Meaningful Life – Joshua Fields Millburn and Ryan Nicodemus (US, 2016)

Succeed – How We Can Reach Our Goals with the Nine Things Successful People Do Differently – Heidi Grant Halvorson, Ph.D. (US, 2010)

The Four Disciplines of Execution – Achieving Your Wildly Important Goals – C McChesney, S Covey, J Huling (US, 2012)

The Happiness Project – Gretchen Rubin (USA, 2009)

The One Goal – Master the Art of Goal Setting, Win Your Inner Battles and Achieve Exceptional Results – Thibaut Meurisse (US, 2017)

The ONE Thing – The surprisingly simple truth behind extraordinary results – Gary Keller with Jay Papasan (US, 2013)

The Secret – Rhonda Byrne (US, 2006)

References

The Seven Habits of Highly Effective People – Restoring the Character Ethic – Steven R Covey (US, 1990)

The Top Five Regrets of the Dying – A Life Transformed by the Dearly Departed – Bronnie Ware (US, 2011)

The Winner's Bible – Rewire Your Brain for Permanent Change – Dr Kerry Spackman (USA, 2009)

The Zigzag Principle – The Goal-Setting Strategy that will Revolutionize Your Business and Your Life – Rich Christiansen (US, 2012)

Thrive – The Third Metric to Redefining Success and Creating a Life of Wellbeing, Wisdom and Wonder – Arianna Huffington (US, 2014)

You are a Badass – How to Stop Doubting Your Greatness and Start Living an Awesome Life – Jen Sincero (US, 2013)

Printed in Great Britain
by Amazon